The Practicing the Way Course

Companion Guide

An Eight-Session Primer on Spiritual Formation

WaterBrook

John Mark Comer and Practicing the Way

Scripture quotations are taken from the Holy Bible, New International Version®, NIV®. Copyright © 1973, 1978, 1984, 2011 by Biblica Inc.™ Used by permission of Zondervan. All rights reserved worldwide. (www.zondervan.com). The "NIV" and "New International Version" are trademarks registered in the United States Patent and Trademark Office by Biblica Inc.™

A WaterBrook Trade Paperback Original

Copyright © 2024 by Practicing the Way

All rights reserved.

Published in the United States by WaterBrook, an imprint of Random House, a division of Penguin Random House LLC.

WATERBROOK and colophon are registered trademarks of Penguin Random House LLC.

Originally self-published by Practicing the Way (practicingtheway.org) in 2024.

Published in association with Yates & Yates, www.yates2.com.

All photos courtesy of Practicing the Way.

Trade Paperback ISBN 978-0-593-60273-7
Ebook ISBN 978-0-593-60274-4

Printed in the United States of America on acid-free paper.

waterbrookmultnomah.com

1st Printing

Most WaterBrook books are available at special quantity discounts for bulk purchase for premiums, fundraising, and corporate and educational needs by organizations, churches, and businesses. Special books or book excerpts also can be created to fit specific needs. For details, contact specialmarketscms @penguinrandomhouse.com.

Contents

PART 01

Getting Started

Welcome

In the fourth century, the desert father St. Sarapion traveled from his monastery in Egypt to visit a woman in the city of Rome. The woman had become widely known for her devotion to Jesus, but, unlike Sarapion, she did not retreat into the desert. She stayed firmly planted in the noise and chaos of urban life.

When Sarapion found her, she was quietly sitting in her room.

He asked her, "Why are you sitting here?"

She answered, "I'm not sitting, I am on a journey."

Following Jesus has long been likened to a spiritual journey. When Jesus invited his first disciples to "follow" him on the "way," he was simultaneously saying that discipleship to him is a lifelong path.

This Course is just a *primer*. It's designed to get you started on the journey of spiritual formation, help you get *unstuck* if you've stalled out, or just guide you into taking your next step. Ultimately, its goal is to train you to live as an apprentice of Jesus: to be with Jesus, become like him, and do as he did.

Whatever prompted you to come on this Course, welcome. We're so happy you're here.

May this experience lay the foundation for a life of apprenticeship to Jesus that you can build on for decades to come.

—John Mark Comer and Practicing the Way

How to Run This Course

A few things you need to know

01   This Course is designed to be done in community, whether with a few friends around a table, with your small group, in a larger class format, or with your entire church.

02   The Course is eight sessions long. We recommend meeting together every week or every other week.

03   You will all need a copy of this Companion Guide. You can purchase a print or ebook version from your preferred book retailer or find a free digital PDF version by signing up at link.practicingtheway.org/course-signup. We recommend the print version so you can stay away from your devices during the practices, as well as take notes during each session. But we realize that digital works better for some.

04   Each session should take about one to two hours, depending on how long you give for discussion and whether you engage in the optional after-video discussion. See the Sample Session on the following page.

Sample session

Here is what a typical session could look like.

Welcome
Welcome the group and open in prayer.

Discussion 01: Practice reflection (15-20 min.)
Process your previous week's practice in community with the questions in the Guide.

Course Video, Part 01 (20 min.)
Watch Part 1 of the video.

Discussion 02: Group conversation (15-30 min.)
Pause the video when indicated for a group-wide conversation.

Course Video, Part 02 (10 min.)
Watch Part 2 of the video.

Discussion 03: After the video (10-15 min.) (Optional)
If you'd like, we have additional questions in the Guide for continued conversation. They are geared toward the coming week's practice.

Prayer to close
Close by praying the liturgy in the Guide, or however you choose.

The Practicing the Way Course is designed to work in a variety of group sizes and environments. For that reason, your gatherings may include additional elements like a meal or worship time or follow a structure slightly different than this sample. Please adapt as you see fit.

The weekly rhythm

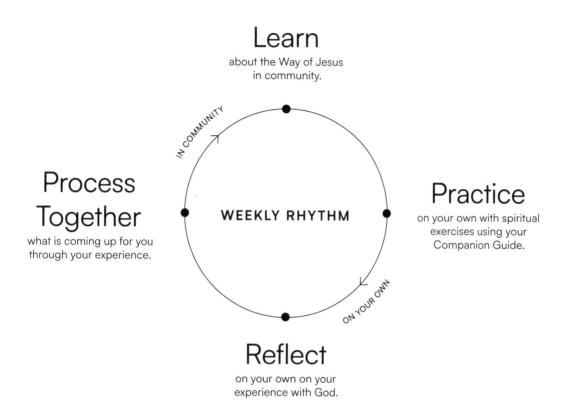

Learn
about the Way of Jesus
in community.

IN COMMUNITY

Process
Together
what is coming up for you
through your experience.

WEEKLY RHYTHM

Practice
on your own with spiritual
exercises using your
Companion Guide.

ON YOUR OWN

Reflect
on your own on your
experience with God.

01 **Learn:** Gather together as a community for an interactive experience of learning about the Way of Jesus through teaching, storytelling, and discussion. Bring your Guide to the session and follow along.

02 **Practice:** On your own, before the next session, go and "put it into practice," as Jesus himself said. We will provide weekly spiritual disciplines and spiritual exercises, as well as recommended resources to go deeper.

03 **Reflect:** Reflection is key to spiritual formation. After your practice and before the next session,

set aside 10 to 15 minutes to reflect on your experience. Reflection questions are included in this Guide at the end of each session.

04 **Process together:** When you come back together, begin by sharing your reflections with your group. This moment is crucial, because we need each other to process our life before God and make sense of our stories. If you are meeting in a larger group, you will need to break into smaller sub-groups for this conversation so everyone has a chance to share.

The *Practicing the Way* book

We highly recommend reading the book *Practicing the Way* by John Mark Comer alongside this Course, as it will greatly enhance your learning experience. Find out more at practicingtheway.org/book.

Each session's readings are laid out in the On Your Own sections in this Guide.

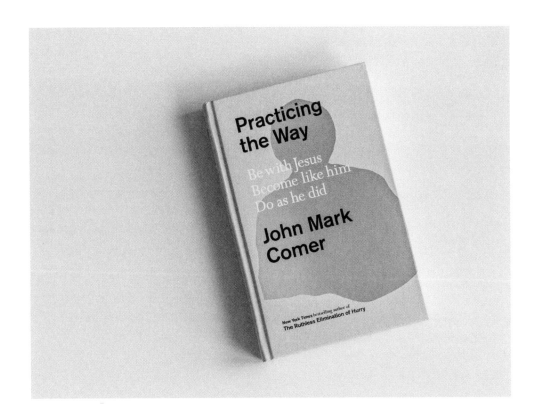

Getting Started

The Spiritual Health Reflection

One final note: Before you begin Session 01, please set aside 20 to 30 minutes and take the Spiritual Health Reflection. This is a self-assessment we developed in partnership with pastors and leading experts in spiritual formation. It's designed to help you reflect on the health of your soul, in order to better name Jesus' invitations to you as you follow the Way.

You can come back to the Spiritual Health Reflection as often as you'd like (we recommend one to two times a year) to chart your growth and continue to move forward on your spiritual journey.

To access the Spiritual Health Reflection, visit practicingtheway.org/reflection, and create an account, and answer the prompt questions slowly and prayerfully.

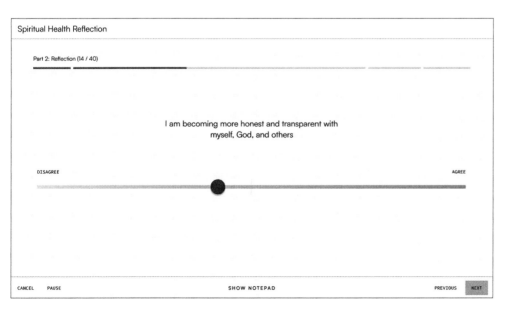

PART 02

The Eight Sessions

Following Jesus

Overview

Who are you following? Everybody is following *somebody*. Put another way: We're all disciples. The question isn't, "Are you a disciple?" but, "*Who* or *what* are you a disciple *of*?" In this session, we explore what it means to be a disciple or apprentice of Jesus.

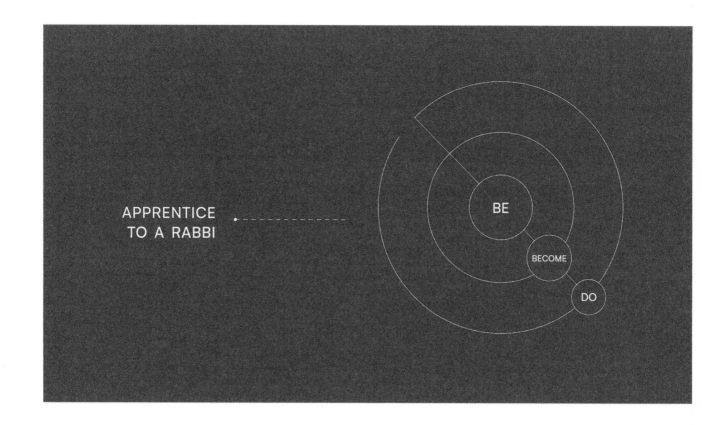

Opening questions

Before we begin our first session, process your thoughts and feelings together as a community as you embark on this Course.

01   What drew you to this Course?

02   What are you looking forward to?

03   Describe in brief your spiritual journey thus far.

Teaching

Scripture

As Jesus walked beside the Sea of Galilee, he saw Simon and his brother Andrew casting a net into the lake, for they were fishermen. "Come, follow me," Jesus said, "and I will send you out to fish for people." At once they left their nets and followed him.

—Mark 1v16-18

Session summary

- Following Jesus is based on the first-century practice of rabbis and apprentices.

- Today, to follow Jesus means to apprentice under him.

- To apprentice under Jesus is to organize your life around three driving goals:

  - Be with Jesus

  - Become like Jesus

  - Do as he did

- Apprenticing under Jesus means practicing a way of life.

- One of the best ways to begin is through a daily prayer rhythm, where you create a time and place for solitude, silence, and prayer.

Teaching notes

Discussion questions

Here are some questions for discussion:

01 What are you hoping Jesus will do in you through this Course?

02 As you look back on your life, who or what has had the greatest impact on your spiritual journey thus far?

03 What do you think is the driving aim of your life? Your top goals and priorities?

04 How can we as a community be praying for you?

Practice notes

As you continue to watch Session 01 together, feel free to take notes here.

After the video

Closing prayer

End your time together by praying this liturgy:

God of love, who seeks and pursues us,
teach us how to seek and pursue you too,
that in our learning anew how to pray,
we may give you what you so deeply long for —
all of us enjoying all of you, forever.
Amen.

OPTIONAL

If you'd like to continue your conversation, here are some additional questions for reflection:

01 When you envision starting your day with silence, solitude, and prayer, what excites you? What challenges you?

02 Think about your week and come up with a plan. When and where will you engage in this practice?

Reflection notes

Feel free to use this page for notes on the optional reflection questions.

Practice

Developing a daily prayer rhythm

We need more than information for transformation. The practices of Jesus (which we'll learn more about in Session 04) help to get the teachings of Jesus into the muscle memory of our bodies. They turn the *idea* of following Jesus into a *reality* in our daily life.

And one of the best ways to begin to "be with Jesus" is by developing a daily prayer rhythm.

There's no "right" way to do this — you may choose to go on an early morning walk with your dog or curl up under a blanket with a cup of tea or sit cross-legged on the floor and breathe deeply. You may pray the Psalms or let a prayer app guide your meditation. You may do this before the sun rises or as it sets.

Whatever you decide, our exercise for Session 01 is to develop a daily time and place to commune with God through the practices of silence, solitude, and prayer.

Here are a few suggestions for your practice:

01   **Find a quiet *place* that is distraction-free.**

   ○ This could be a corner in your home or a nearby park. Find somewhere that you can focus and be at peace.

02   **Find a quiet *time*.**

   ○ For many people, first thing upon waking is the best possible time to do this; but for you, it may be before bed, or while your baby is napping mid-morning, or on a lunch break.

   ○ The general rule is: *Give God your best time of the day*.

03   **Come to quiet.**

   ○ If at all possible (unless you're using an app such as Lectio 365 or Pray as You Go to guide your prayer time), put your phone away in another room. Start with a few deep breaths ... in and out of your nose, and let your mind and body calm down.

○ This may take a few minutes. You're not in a hurry. And then ...

04 Open your heart to God in prayer.

○ Again, there's no "right" way to pray. But you don't have to start from scratch.

○ For thousands of years, followers of Jesus have used the Psalms for daily prayer. The Psalms are a collection of poetic prayers found in the middle of the Bible, and they were designed to be *prayed*, not just read.

○ You can pray one psalm or pray a few; it's up to you. You can start in Psalm 1 and keep going to pray a selection. If you want to pray one psalm, here are some we suggest you start with: Psalms 1, 23, 37, 40, 42-43, 63, 84, 86, 103, and 139.

This whole exercise can be done in five minutes, or it can easily take up to an hour — again, that's up to you. The key is: Start where you are, not where you feel you "should" be. If two or three minutes is all you can make happen, start *there* and take the next step.

If you didn't get a chance to take the Spiritual Health Reflection before Session 01, please remember to do so before you come back together. Visit practicingtheway.org/reflection, create an account, and answer the prompt questions slowly and prayerfully.

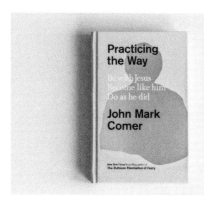

This session's reading

For this session, we're reading "Apprentice to Jesus," in *Practicing the Way* by John Mark Comer, pp. 1-31.

Resources to go deeper

If you're interested in learning more about what it means to be an apprentice of Jesus or growing in your practice of prayer, here are some more resources to consider.

Recommended reading

- *The Deeply Formed Life* by our guest, Rich Villodas
- *The Great Omission* by Dallas Willard
- *Walking in the Dust of Rabbi Jesus* by Lois Tverberg
- *Praying like Monks, Living like Fools* by Tyler Staton
- *Time for God* by Jacques Philippe

Recommended listening

- Rich Villodas' teaching series, The Deeply Formed Life from New Life Fellowship: link.practicingtheway.org/course-s1
- The Practicing the Way Vision Series from Bridgetown Church: bridgetown.church/series/practicing-the-way
- Episode 01 of the Practicing the Way podcast: link.practicingtheway.org/course-s1b

Additional resources

- The Prayer Practice from Practicing the Way: practicingtheway.org/prayer. If you'd like to learn more about the practice of prayer, you can run the Prayer Practice, a four-session experience designed to integrate the practice of prayer into your regular life.

Guest bio

Our guest this session was Rich Villodas, author, speaker, and lead pastor of New Life Fellowship, a large, multiracial church in Queens, New York. To learn more, visit richvillodas.com or read his book, *The Deeply Formed Life.*

Practice reflection

Reflection is a key component in our spiritual formation. Like practice, it allows what we learn to become a part of who we are.

Before your next time together, take five to ten minutes to journal out your answers to the following three questions.

01 **What was most challenging about practicing a rhythm of prayer?**

02 **What is something you enjoyed about it?**

03 **What are you hoping for as you continue this rhythm of prayer?**

Formation
Part 01

Overview

Spiritual formation isn't a Christian thing or even a religious thing; it's a *human* thing. To be human is to grow, to mature, to adapt over time. Formation is simply the process by which our "spirit," or inner person, is formed into a particular shape or character. Over a lifetime, we are spiritually formed by a complex alchemy of genetic inheritance, family patterns, childhood wounds, education, habits, decisions, relationships, environments, and more.

The problem is, most of our spiritual formation is unintentional. *It just happens.* And often, we are "conform[ed] to the pattern of this world," *more* than "transformed by the renewing of [our] mind."*

---

* Romans 12v2

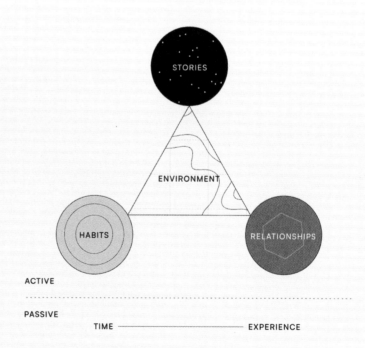

Unintentional Spiritual Formation

STORIES

ENVIRONMENT

HABITS

RELATIONSHIPS

ACTIVE

PASSIVE

TIME ——————— EXPERIENCE

Practice reflection

Before we begin Session 02, break up into small groups and share your reflections on last session's practice of prayer.

01 What was most challenging about practicing a rhythm of prayer?

02 What is something you enjoyed about it?

03 What are you hoping for as you continue this rhythm of prayer?

Teaching

Scripture

Do not conform to the pattern of this world, but be transformed by the renewing of your mind.

—Romans 12v2

Session summary

- Spiritual formation isn't a Christian thing; it's a *human* thing.

- We are formed by a complex web of forces, but especially by:

    ◦ Habits

    ◦ Relationships

    ◦ The stories we believe

    ◦ Environment

    ◦ Time

    ◦ Experience

- Most of our formation is unintentional.

- Some of the most important questions to reflect on are:

    ◦ Who am I becoming?

    ◦ Am I being intentional about who I am becoming?

- One of the best ways to do this is through a Formation Audit.

Teaching notes

Discussion questions

Pause the video and take some time to process together as a community.

Here are some questions for discussion:

01 What habits do you keep in your daily and weekly life? How might they be shaping you?

02 Who are the most important people in your life? What do those relationships look like?

03 As you reflect on your own journey, what stories have shaped the way you view the world? Where did these stories originate?

04 Did God reveal anything new to you in this session that you want to say more about?

Practice notes

As you continue to watch Session 02 together, feel free to take notes here.

After the video

Closing prayer

End your time together by praying this liturgy:

Good Creator, who made our inmost parts,
you see more of us than we do,
you know us better than we ever will,
and yet you call us "beloved";
give us courage to see ourselves in the light,
to be honest with who we are, and what we're not,
that in our being fully seen by you,
we may be transformed ever more greatly,
by your love, into your holy image.
Amen.

OPTIONAL

If you'd like to continue your conversation, here are some additional questions
for reflection:

01 When you consider the list of forces that can unintentionally form us,
    does anything surprise you or stand out to you?

02 When do you plan to set aside time for your Formation Audit? Is there
    anything coming up for you as you think about doing the audit?

Reflection notes

Feel free to use this page for notes on the optional reflection questions.

Practice

Formation Audit

Practice helps the information we take in become a part of who we are and transform our lives.

Our exercise for this session is to take an inventory of all the forces that are currently forming you.

01　**This is one of the longest exercises in this Course, and we recommend you carve out a quiet time and place to spend ample time in thoughtful reflection and prayer.**

02　**Invite the Spirit of Jesus to come and illuminate your mind, to silence the voice of the evil one, and to "give you the Spirit of wisdom and revelation, so that you may know him better," and that "the eyes of your heart may be enlightened."***

03　**Remember to answer *honestly* and *nonjudgmentally*. You will likely feel your heart drift toward shame and denial, both of which will sabotage the effectiveness of this exercise.**

04　**Above all, do this exercise *with God*. Slowly and prayerfully, and with your heart at peace.**

---

* Ephesians 1v17-18

Habits — What habits make up your everyday life? Write out your habits.

Morning routine:

_____

_____

_____

_____

Activities of a typical workday:

_____

_____

_____

_____

Evening routine:

_____

_____

_____

_____

Activities of a typical weekend:

_____

_____

_____

_____

Reflection: How do you think your habits are shaping you as a person? (See the two lists on page 44 for a list of possible effects.)

_____

_____

_____

_____

Relationships — What relationships make up most of your life?

Family:

_____

_____

_____

Friends:

_____

_____

_____

Work:

_____

_____

_____

Community:

_____

_____

_____

Other:

_____

_____

_____

Reflection: How are these people shaping you as a person? The key questions to ask are: What kind of person do I become when I'm around this person? What do they draw out in me or suppress in me?

_____

_____

_____

_____

Stories you believe — What are the "stories" you have come to believe?

What stories do you believe about God? (What is he like/not like? How does he feel toward you?)

_____

_____

_____

_____

What stories do you believe about yourself? (How does God see you? How do others see you? What kind of person are you? What do you see for your future?)

_____

_____

_____

_____

What stories do you believe about happiness? (What do you think will make you most happy and peaceful? Is it God? Money? Marriage? Success? Vacation?)

_____

_____

_____

_____

What stories do you believe about the meaning of life? (What do you think matters most? Perhaps your career? Family? Health? Something else?)

_____

_____

_____

_____

Reflection: What are the core stories of my life? Are they forming me as a person?

_____

_____

_____

Environment — What are the cultural distinctives of my environment?

City: What is my city like? What is it known for?

_____

_____

_____

Nation: What is my nation like? What are its highest cultural values?

_____

_____

_____

Generation: What are my generation's values?

_____

_____

_____

Digital algorithm: What are the algorithms feeding me news, information, and social connection like?

_____

_____

_____

Ethnic and/or socio-economic group: What are the values and cultural norms and expectations of my cultural heritage and socio-economic class?

_____

_____

_____

Reflection: How am I being formed or deformed by the cultural forces that are "normal" in my city/nation/generation/social media feed, but possibly far from the vision of Jesus?

_____

_____

_____

Experience — What life experiences have most shaped me into who I am today?

Family of origin: What is my family like? What are its highest values? Deepest dysfunctions? Greatest legacy?

_____

_____

_____

Traumatic events: Have I experienced a traumatic event? What story has my body wordlessly learned from that trauma?

_____

_____

_____

Key experiences: What are the key moments on the timeline of my life that have altered the trajectory of my story?

_____

_____

_____

Spiritual autobiography: What are the key moments of my spiritual journey thus far?

_____

_____

_____

Reflection: How have my experiences formed and deformed me over the years? Where do I still need healing? What do I need to never forget and hold on to? What am I still missing?

_____

_____

_____

Possible effects of following "the pattern of this world":

- Stress
- Hurry
- Anxiety
- Fear
- Insecurity
- Hypervigilance
- Jealousy
- Anger
- Irritation
- Impatience
- Resentment

- Outrage
- Pride
- Distraction
- Numbness
- Overwhelm
- Exhaustion
- Discouragement
- Loneliness
- Isolation
- Shame
- Division

- Disconnection
- Lying
- Dirty speech
- Sarcasm
- Put-downs
- Dishonor of authority
- Contempt
- Careerism
- Overwork
- Materialism
- Discontent

- Debt
- Laziness
- Alcoholism
- Addiction
- Substance abuse
- Impulsiveness
- Lust
- Pornography
- Racism
- Bigotry

Possible markers of following the Way of God's Kingdom:

- Love
- Joy
- Peace
- Patience
- Kindness
- Gentleness
- Faithfulness
- Self-control
- Faith
- Hope

- Unhurried living
- Simplicity of life
- Calm
- Generosity
- Contentment
- Freedom
- Warmth and affection
- Relational connection
- Community
- Sense of belonging

- Equity
- Diversity
- Trust
- Acceptance
- Authenticity
- Honesty
- Integrity
- Harmony
- Vulnerability
- Compassion

- Restfulness
- Diligence
- A sense of meaning and purpose
- A clear sense of direction
- Creativity
- Growth

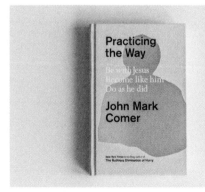

This session's reading

For this session, we're reading "Goal #1: Be with Jesus," in *Practicing the Way* by John Mark Comer, pp. 32-63.

Resources to go deeper

If you're interested in learning more about spiritual formation, here are some more resources to consider.

Recommended reading

- *Invitation to a Journey* by M. Robert Mulholland
- *You Are What You Love* by James K.A. Smith
- *Beautiful Resistance* by our guest, Jon Tyson

Recommended listening

- The Way teaching series from Jon Tyson and Church of the City New York:
  link.practicingtheway.org/course-s2
- Episode 02 of the Practicing the Way podcast: link.practicingtheway.org/course-s2b

Guest bio

Our guest this session was Jon Tyson, author, teacher, and pastor of Church of the City
New York in Manhattan. To learn more, visit jontyson.co or church.nyc.

Practice reflection

Reflection is a key component in our spiritual formation. Like practice, it allows what we learn to become a part of who we are.

Before your next time together, take five to ten minutes to journal out your answers to the following three questions.

01   **What did you find helpful about taking the Formation Audit?**

02   **When you consider the ways you are being unintentionally formed, what felt most challenging?**

03   **Did anything surprise you?**

Formation
Part 02

Overview

In the last session, we explored the reality that we're *already being formed* by our habits, relationships, environments, and more. Therefore, all formation in the Way of Jesus is *counter-formation*. As apprentices of Jesus, our goal is to intentionally slow our lives down to find deep joy in walking with Jesus.

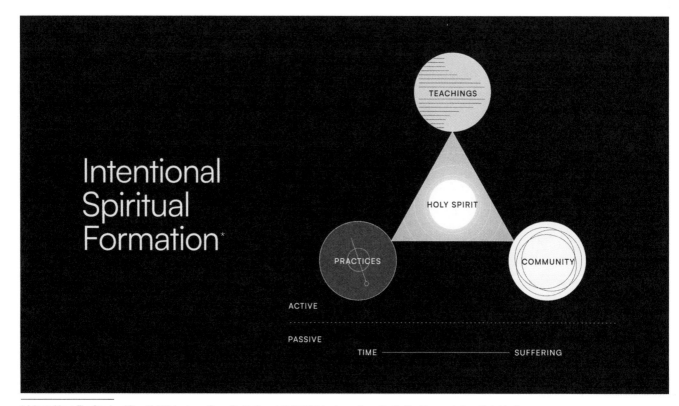

Intentional Spiritual Formation*

TEACHINGS

HOLY SPIRIT

PRACTICES

COMMUNITY

ACTIVE

PASSIVE

TIME ———————— SUFFERING

* Adapted from *The Good and Beautiful Life* by James Bryan Smith. Copyright © 2009 by James Bryan Smith. Used by permission of InterVarsity Press, P.O. Box 1400, Downers Grove, IL 60515, USA, www.ivpress.com.

Practice reflection

Before we begin Session 03, break up into small groups and share your reflections on last session's Formation Audit exercise.

01   What did you find helpful about taking the Formation Audit?

02   When you consider the ways you are being unintentionally formed, what felt most challenging?

03   Did anything surprise you?

Teaching

Scripture

The apprentice is not above the rabbi, but everyone who is fully trained will be like their rabbi.

—Luke 6v40*

Session summary

- We may desire to become more like Jesus, but feel stuck.

- The problem is that we don't know *how* to become like Jesus.

- We need a training program — a reliable pathway to transformation.

- We find this in the Way of Jesus, where we are formed by:

    - The Practices

    - Community

    - Teaching

    - The Holy Spirit

- Formation happens over time and through suffering.

- And one of the best ways to begin to change is to replace an unhealthy habit with the practice of reading Scripture daily.

---

* Key words adapted

Teaching notes

Discussion questions

Here are some questions for discussion:

01 Have you ever had a moment in your discipleship where you felt "stuck," whether in habits, in unhealthy emotional patterns, or in your relationship to God?

02 With the paradigm of intentional spiritual formation in mind, how have you participated in your own formation over the years?

03 How have you understood the Holy Spirit's role in spiritual formation?

04 Have you had an experience of intentionally opening your pain and suffering to God? What did God produce in your formation through that experience?

Practice notes

After the video

Closing prayer

End your time together by praying this liturgy:

Thank you, Father, for your word,
for your Son who speaks it to us,
and for your Spirit who illumines it within.
Teach us how to read it with you,
that we may learn to love its wisdom,
goodness, and truth, growing in your Way.
Amen.

OPTIONAL

If you'd like to continue your conversation, here are some additional questions for reflection:

01 How do you currently engage with Scripture?

02 What comes up for you when you think about starting your day
with a rhythm of reading Scripture? What would you like to share
with your group?

03 As a group, talk about your plan for this week. Will you use a reading plan
or a particular book of the Bible? What time and setting is best for you?
(Reading plan ideas are listed at the end of the Practice section.)

Reflection notes

Feel free to use this page for notes on the optional reflection questions.

Practice

Daily reading of Scripture

Information alone doesn't produce transformation. To grow, let's put what we've learned into practice.

Last session, you conducted a Formation Audit. You made a list of all your habits and relationships, and then you attempted to connect the dots between them and your formation or deformation.

Did you identify any habits or relationships or stories that seem to be having a negative effect on you?

This session's practice is to take the next step and replace an old habit with a new practice.

And if it's not already a part of your daily life with God, we invite you to begin the practice of reading Scripture. The best way to do this is likely to *add* it to the daily prayer rhythm you began two sessions ago. Hopefully by now you're learning to carve out a quiet place and time, and come to quiet before God. A next step could be to integrate the reading of Scripture into your daily rhythm in a prayerful, peaceful way.

Here are a few reminders from the Prayer Practice:

01 **Identify a quiet *place* that is distraction-free.**

- ○ This could be a corner in your home or a nearby park. Find somewhere that you can focus and be at peace.

- ○ If at all possible (unless you're using an app to read or follow a reading plan), put your phone away in another room.

02 **Identify a quiet *time*.**

- ○ For many people, first thing upon waking is the best possible time to do this; but for you, it may be before bed, or while your baby is napping mid-morning, or on a lunch break.

- ○ The general rule is: *Give God your best time of the day.*

03 **Come to quiet.**

- Start with a few deep breaths ... in and out of your nose, and let your mind and body calm down.

- This may take a few minutes. You're not in a hurry.

- And then ...

04 **Open your heart to God in prayer.**

- Again, there's no "right" way to pray. But you don't have to start from scratch.

05 **Read Scripture.**

- Choose a section of Scripture or follow a Bible reading plan suggested in the Resources to Go Deeper section.

- As you read, you might want to notice what resonates with you, what emotionally lifts off the page and into your heart.

- Your goal is to listen for Jesus' voice coming to you.

This whole exercise can be done in five minutes, or it can easily take up to an hour — again, that's up to you. The key is: Start where you *are*, not where you feel you "should" be.

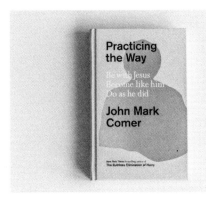

This session's reading

For this session, we're reading "Goal #2: Become like him," in *Practicing the Way* by John Mark Comer, pp. 64-117.

Resources to go deeper

If you're interested in learning more about intentional spiritual formation or the practice of reading Scripture, here are some more resources to consider.

BibleProject

We highly recommend the amazing videos and resources from our friends at BibleProject, who are all about helping people engage with Scripture as a unified story that leads to Jesus.

On the topic of Scripture, we recommend the following:

- For a taste, the Genesis 1 video:

  link.practicingtheway.org/course-s3a

- On reading Scripture, the How to Read the Bible video series: link.practicingtheway.org/course-s3b

- To go deeper, the Paradigm podcast:

  bibleproject.com/podcast/series/paradigm

BibleProject reading plans, bibleproject.com/reading-plans, and some suggestions:

- *The Character of God*   6 days
- *Introduction to the Christian Faith*   8 days
- *What Gives You Hope?*   7 days
- *Trusting God Through Suffering*   6 days
- *One Story That Leads to Jesus*   1 year

Recommended reading

- *The Renovation of the Heart* by Dallas Willard
- *Liturgy of the Ordinary* by our guest, Tish Harrison Warren
- *Shaped by the Word* by M. Robert Mulholland

Recommended listening

- The Scripture Practice teaching series by Bridgetown Church:

  bridgetown.church/series/scripture

- The Year of Biblical Literacy by Reality San Francisco: realitysf.com/bible

- Episode 03 of the Practicing the Way podcast:

  link.practicingtheway.org/course-s3

Additional resources

- The Scripture Practice from Practicing the Way: practicingtheway.org/scripture (coming soon). If you'd like to learn more about the practice of reading Scripture, you can run the Scripture Practice, a four-session experience designed to integrate the practice of reading Scripture into your regular life.

Guest bio

Our guest this session was Tish Harrison Warren, author and priest in the Anglican Church in North America. Learn more about her and her work at tishharrisonwarren.com.

Practice reflection

Reflection is a key component in our spiritual formation. Like practice, it allows what we learn to become a part of who we are.

Before your next time together, take five to ten minutes to journal out your answers to the following four questions.

01 How did your practice of reading Scripture go following the last session?

02 Where did you experience resistance in this practice?

03 In what ways did you encounter God in it?

04 Did anything surprise you?

The Practices

Overview

The practices of Jesus are essential to our spiritual formation. They are how we do what we *can* do — Sabbath, pray, read Scripture — to make space for God to transform us into the kind of people who can do what we currently *cannot* do — live and love like Jesus. And they slow our busy lives down to the pace and presence of "the God of peace."

SABBATH	PRAYER	FASTING
SOLITUDE	GENEROSITY	SCRIPTURE
COMMUNITY	SERVICE	WITNESS

Practice reflection

Before we begin Session 04, break up into small groups and share your reflections on last session's practice of reading Scripture.

01 How did your practice of reading Scripture go following the last session?

02 Where did you experience resistance in this practice?

03 In what ways did you encounter God in it?

04 Did anything surprise you?

Teaching

Scripture

Very early in the morning, while it was still dark, Jesus got up, left the house and went off to a solitary place, where he prayed.

—Mark 1v35

Session summary

- The Practices are disciplines based on the lifestyle of Jesus that create time and space for us to access the presence and power of the Spirit and, in doing so, be transformed from the inside out.

- Practices are a means to an end: to live and love like Jesus.

- We approach deeper changes in our life indirectly, not directly, by practicing ancient disciplines that open us up to God to change us at the deepest level.

- Practices are not the whole of the spiritual life, they are just one part of it.

- They are essential for those who desire to be transformed to become more like Jesus.

- One of the most important practices for our age of exhaustion is Sabbath — a full day set aside to stop, rest, delight, and worship.

The Practices

Sabbath	Solitude	Community
Prayer	Generosity	Service
Fasting	Scripture	Witness

Teaching notes

As you watch Session 04 together, feel free to use this page to take notes.

Discussion questions

Pause the video and take some time to process together as a community.

Here are some questions for discussion:

01 What's your experience with the spiritual disciplines? What practices have you engaged with in your spiritual journey?

02 If the practices are the means, what do you understand the end of the spiritual life to be?

03 Who has most reflected God's love to you? Where did you see the life of Jesus at work in them?

04 Do you practice any kind of Sabbath or day of rest? Or is this a new discipline for you?

Practice notes

As you continue to watch Session 04 together, feel free to take notes here.

After the video

Closing prayer

End your time together by praying this liturgy:

With the stillness of this night,
we offer the stillness of our beings —
our minds, our hands, our souls;
that in the quiet of your love
we may again hear you whisper,
"You are my beloved."

OPTIONAL

If you'd like to continue your conversation, here are some additional questions
for reflection:

01   What comes to mind for you when you think about ceasing some things
and embracing what gives life?

02   Talk about your plan with your group. When and where will you
practice Sabbath?

Reflection notes

Feel free to use this page for notes on the optional reflection questions.

Practice

Sabbath

To grow, we need more than content; we need real, embodied practice.

In our age of exhaustion, Sabbath is one of the most neglected and most crucial of all the practices of Jesus. But it can be daunting to begin, as it's an entire 24 hours, and you're swimming against the current of our entire culture. Powerful forces keep us tethered to our devices, distractions, and the endless queue of work and responsibilities.

So, start small. If a full Sabbath day is too much for you, start with a Sabbath morning or afternoon. Set aside a few hours after church or early on a Saturday to embrace the four movements of Sabbath: stop, rest, delight, and worship.

Four things to keep in mind as you begin:

01 **Begin by connecting with God.** The Hebrew people called this "sanctifying the day," setting it aside from the other six days. You could light two candles, or pray a psalm or share a meal or begin with Sunday worship at your church. But have a clear ritual or moment with God that *begins* and *ends* your Sabbath time.

02 **If you can, spend part of the day with your family or friends who follow Jesus.** You could throw a Sabbath meal or just spend unhurried time in conversation.

03 **Do whatever makes you come alive in God.** Nap, read poetry, play basketball with your kids. Pursue whatever activities make you feel joyful, rested, and alive to God; whatever it is you do that makes your heart spontaneously burst into gratitude and worship.

04 **Keep at it.** Integrating Sabbath keeping into your life usually takes months or years, not weeks. Just start small and aim at joy.

Here's a short guide to planning out your next Sabbath.

- When will you Sabbath? (Include your start and end time)

- How will you mark the beginning and end of your Sabbath time?
  (A ritual or liturgy or prayerful moment)

- What will you do with your devices?

- What do you need to do to prepare? (Grocery shopping, emails, errands, work tasks, phone calls, etc.)

- How will you include friends and family?

- What will you do to fill your heart with joy and peace?

- How can you create Sabbath for those who have none?

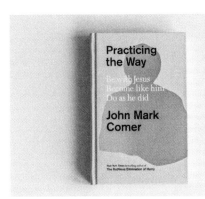

This session's reading

For this session, we're reading "Goal #3: Do as he did," in *Practicing the Way* by John Mark Comer, pp. 118-155.

Resources to go deeper

If you're interested in learning more about the keystone practice of Sabbath, here are some more resources to consider.

Recommended reading

- *The Sabbath* by Dan Allender
- *Keeping the Sabbath Wholly* by Marva J. Dawn
- *The Sabbath* by Abraham Joshua Heschel
- *Subversive Sabbath* by A.J. Swoboda

Recommended listening

- Sabbath Rhythms sermon by Rich Villodas:
  link.practicingtheway.org/course-s4a
- Subversive Sabbath sermon by A.J. Swoboda:
  link.practicingtheway.org/course-s4b
- Rest Must Be Stronger Than Exhaustion sermon
  by Jon Tyson:
  link.practicingtheway.org/course-s4c
- The Sabbath series from the Rule of Life podcast:
  link.practicingtheway.org/course-s4d

- The Sabbath series from Bridgetown Church:
  bridgetown.church/series/sabbath
- Episode 04 of the Practicing the Way podcast:
  link.practicingtheway.org/course-s4e

Additional resources

- The Sabbath Practice from Practicing the Way:
  practicingtheway.org/sabbath. If you'd like to
  learn more about the practice of Sabbath, you
  can run the Sabbath Practice, a four-session
  experience designed to integrate the practice of
  Sabbath into your regular life.

Guest bio

Our guest this session was Jane Willard. Jane is a therapist, spiritual director, author, and widow of Dallas Willard. She works with organizations and publishers to carry on Dallas' message of Kingdom living in the present.

Practice reflection

Reflection is a key component in our spiritual formation. Like practice, it allows what we learn to become a part of who we are.

Before your next time together, take five to ten minutes to journal out your answers to the following four questions.

01   What was challenging about your Sabbath practice?

02   Where did you feel delight in your practice?

03   Where did you most experience God's nearness?

04   Is there anything different you would like to try related to the practice of Sabbath?

Meeting God in Pain and Suffering

Overview

Jesus once said, "In this world you will have trouble."* Pain and suffering are inevitable in this life. Often, when we begin to practice the disciplines, the unhealed wounds of a lifetime rise to the surface of our hearts. Everything in us wants to run in the opposite direction — to deny, detach, or drug our pain. But the invitation of Jesus is to meet him *in* our pain, and let it become the crucible of our formation.

---

* John 16v33

Practice reflection

Before we begin Session 05, break up into small groups and share your reflections on last session's practice of Sabbath.

01   What was challenging about your Sabbath practice?

02   Where did you feel delight in your practice?

03   Where did you most experience God's nearness?

04   Is there anything different you would like to try related to
the practice of Sabbath?

Teaching

Scripture

Then Jesus went with his disciples to a place called Gethsemane, and he said to them, "Sit here while I go over there and pray." He took Peter and the two sons of Zebedee along with him, and he began to be sorrowful and troubled. Then he said to them, "My soul is overwhelmed with sorrow to the point of death. Stay here and keep watch with me." Going a little farther, he fell with his face to the ground and prayed, "My Father, if it is possible, may this cup be taken from me. Yet not as I will, but as you will."

—Matthew 26v36-39

Session summary

- The practices are not a religious formula to habit-stack our way into spiritual formation.

- When we slow down and come to quiet before God, often the first thing that comes up is emotional pain, as our soul begins to process and discharge all the pain and suffering of our life.

- There are three primary ways people deal with pain:

  ○ Deny

  ○ Detach

  ○ Drug

- The Jesus way is to meet God in our pain.

- Left unhealed, emotional pain can sabotage our transformation. But if we open it to God, it can become the secret to our transformation.

Spiritual bypassing
A tendency to use spiritual ideas and practices to sidestep or avoid facing unresolved emotional issues, psychological wounds, and unfinished developmental tasks.[*]

Emotional maturity
You're aware of your feelings, but you're not run by your feelings.

Spiritual maturity
The ability and willingness to know and do the will of God.

---

* John Welwood, "Principles of Inner Work: Psychological and Spiritual," *Journal of Transpersonal Psychology* 16, no. 1 (1984).

Teaching notes

Discussion questions

Pause the video and take some time to process together as a community.

Here are some questions for discussion:

01 Can you tell one story of a painful experience you've been through that has been used for good in your formation?

02 How have you experienced God in times of pain and suffering?

03 Which of the three responses to emotional pain are you most inclined toward: deny, detach, or drug? What has that looked like in your life?

04 What could it look like for you to reorient yourself to the pain in your life as an opportunity to be formed by God?

Practice notes

As you continue to watch Session 05 together, feel free to take notes here.

After the video

Closing prayer

End your time together by praying this liturgy:

God of Gethsemane, who experiences
and knows the pain of our condition,
help us turn to you in the ache of our emotions
when the day has turned to darkness,
that we may know the liberation of your
transforming love, not only by the calm
water's edge, but when we're traveling on
the waters of the storms that life brings.
Amen.

OPTIONAL

If you'd like to continue your conversation, here are some additional questions for reflection:

01 How familiar are you with noticing and naming your feelings?

02 As you consider the spiritual exercise of noticing and naming your feelings in prayer, what comes up for you?

03 Come up with a plan for your practice this week. When will you try the exercise?

Reflection notes

Feel free to use this page for notes on the optional reflection questions.

Practice

Noticing and naming your emotions

Let's put this teaching into practice, so that what we're learning can become part of who we are.

The journey into emotional health involves learning to notice and name our emotions in the presence of God.

When we notice and name our feelings, they have less power over us. If you were to name a painful emotion like fear, anger, disappointment, or jealousy, a brain scan would show that your very act of naming it helps to process and quiet that emotion. This is why psychiatrist Dan Siegel encourages us to "name it to tame it."

This session's spiritual exercise is a simple template for prayer designed to notice and name your feelings and offer them to God in prayer.

- Find a quiet, distraction-free place and time.

- Put away your phone or any devices, and settle into a comfortable but alert position.

- Take a few minutes to breathe and center your awareness in God's presence. And then do the following:

01 **Notice:** Now that you are centered in your body and in God, begin to let yourself feel. Let whatever is in you come up. Just notice it. Don't fight it or run away from it or feel guilty about it or judge it — just notice it. Let the feeling be.

02 **Name:** Then name the emotion and be as specific as possible. You may want to use the following list of emotions. Just pick out one to three words from the Feelings list on the following page that put language to what you're experiencing in your body.

03 **Feel:** Just sit in those feelings. Sink into them. Normally, we turn away from them and run in the opposite direction. Instead, turn and face them, like you would an ocean wave, and let it wash over you and then pass you by.

04 **Offer it to God:** Remember and follow Jesus' Gethsemane Prayer.

  ○ Give God your feelings — Tell him what you are feeling, with no filter.

  ○ Give God your desires — Tell him what you really want, good or bad.

  ○ Give God your trust — Surrender your heart again to him. Stop grasping for control and yield yourself to God and his will for your life. You may want to pray Jesus' own prayer, "Not my will, but yours be done."

You can do this exercise one time before the next session, or every day. It's also an exercise you can practice for the rest of your life, to open deeper and deeper parts of your inner world to God.

Feelings list*

Happy	Sad	Angry	Scared	Confused
Admired	Alienated	Abused	Afraid	Ambivalent
Alive	Ashamed	Aggravated	Alarmed	Awkward
Appreciated	Burdened	Agitated	Anxious	Baffled
Assured	Condemned	Anguished	Appalled	Bewildered
Cheerful	Crushed	Annoyed	Apprehensive	Bothered
Confident	Defeated	Betrayed	Awed	Constricted
Content	Dejected	Cheated	Concerned	Directionless
Delighted	Demoralized	Coerced	Defensive	Disorganized
Determined	Depressed	Controlled	Desperate	Distracted
Ecstatic	Deserted	Deceived	Doubtful	Doubtful
Elated	Despised	Disgusted	Fearful	Flustered
Encouraged	Devastated	Dismayed	Frantic	Foggy
Energized	Disappointed	Displeased	Full of Dread	Hesitant
Enthusiastic	Discarded	Dominated	Guarded	Immobilized
Excited	Discouraged	Enraged	Horrified	Misunderstood
Exuberant	Disgraced	Exasperated	Impatient	Perplexed
Flattered	Disheartened	Exploited	Insecure	Puzzled
Fortunate	Disillusioned	Frustrated	Intimidated	Stagnant
Fulfilled	Dismal	Fuming	Nervous	Surprised

* Mark Gilson et al., *Overcoming Depression: Thoughts and Depression: The T of the BEAST* (Oxford: Oxford University Press, 2009), https://www.ndapandas.org/wp-content/uploads/archive/Documents/News/FeelingsWordList.pdf. Reproduced with permission of the Licensor through PLSclear.

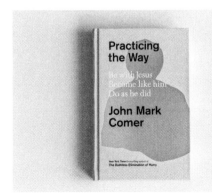

This session's reading

For this session, we're reading "How? A Rule of Life," in *Practicing the Way* by John Mark Comer, pp. 156-205.

Resources to go deeper

If you're interested in growing even more in your practice of meeting God in pain and suffering, here are some more resources to consider.

Recommended reading

- *Emotionally Healthy Spirituality* by Pete Scazzero
- *Untangle Your Emotions* by Jennie Allen
- *The Human Condition* by Thomas Keating

Recommended listening

- The Emotionally Healthy Discipleship Course: link.practicingtheway.org/course-s5
- In This World You Will Have Trouble teaching series from Bridgetown Church: bridgetown.church/series/in-this-world

Guest bio

Our guest this session was Hakeem Bradley. Hakeem is a speaker, pastor, and teacher, and is on the scholarship team at BibleProject, a nonprofit organization committed to creating digital resources that explore the Bible as a unified story that points to Jesus. To learn more about Hakeem, visit hakeembradley.com.

Practice reflection

Reflection is a key component in our spiritual formation. Like practice, it allows what we learn to become a part of who we are.

Before your next time together, take five to ten minutes to journal out your answers to the following three questions.

01 **What was your experience of noticing and naming your feelings before God like? Where did you feel delight in your practice?**

02 **What were the most common feelings that came up for you? Was anything a surprise to you?**

03 **Where did you most experience God's nearness in this practice?**

Healing from Sin

Overview

Jesus once said, "It is not the healthy who need a doctor, but the sick. I have not come to call the righteous, but sinners."* He likened sin to a disease and himself to a healer. Based on this text, ancient Christians called Jesus "the doctor of the soul."

And trying to go on the spiritual journey of discipleship without healing from sin is like trying to run a marathon with a broken leg — you're not going to get very far, and it's not going to be very fun.

A key step in our apprenticeship to Jesus is healing from sin.

---

* Mark 2v17

DIMENSION / 2
SIN / Done to us

Practice reflection

Before we begin Session 06, break up into small groups and share your reflections on last session's exercise of noticing and naming your feelings in prayer.

01   What was your experience of noticing and naming your feelings before God like? Where did you feel delight in your practice?

02   What were the most common feelings that came up for you? Was anything a surprise to you?

03   Where did you most experience God's nearness in this practice?

Teaching

Scripture

It is not the healthy who need a doctor, but the sick. I have not come to call the righteous, but sinners.

—Mark 2v17

Session summary

- A key aspect of the spiritual journey is healing from sin.

- Three dimensions to sin:

    - Sin done *by* us

    - Sin done *to* us

    - And sin done *around* us

- Four layers of sin we move through in our healing:*

    - Gross sins

    - Conscious sins

    - Unconscious sins

    - Attachments

- Our part in the healing of sin is the practice of confession.

---

* M. Robert Mulholland, *Invitation to a Journey: A Road Map for Spiritual Formation* (Downers Grove: IVP, 2016).

Teaching notes

In-session reflection exercise

Pause the video and take a few minutes in the quiet to journal through the following questions:

01   What do you believe about how God sees you and your sin?

02   What came up for you as we talked about sin?

03   Is there anyone you need to forgive or ask for forgiveness from, including God?

Discussion questions

Now take some time to process together as a community, sharing with your small group whatever you're comfortable with in response to the following:

Here are some questions for discussion:

01   Growing up, what was your understanding of sin and God's response to it?

02   When you sin, what do you normally do?

03   As you think about your sin patterns, what attachments or idols are you clinging to in your pursuit of happiness?

04   In light of this teaching, what steps may God be inviting you to take toward healing?

Practice notes

As you continue to watch Session 06 together, feel free to take notes here.

After the video

Closing prayer

End your time together by praying this liturgy:

Loving God, we open ourselves to you
and confess all that we have and have not done,
both consciously and unconsciously,
in opposition to your goodness.
Help us to live more openly with you,
that in our being seen in all,
we may also be healed in all,
growing in your love.
Amen.

OPTIONAL

If you'd like to continue your conversation, here are some additional questions
for reflection:

01 **What comes up for you as you consider this session's exercise
in confession?**

02 **Is there someone who comes to mind when you consider practicing
confession? Or would you be open to partnering with someone in
your group?**

03 **What steps do you need to take to set yourself up to practice
confession this week?**

Reflection notes

Feel free to use this page for notes on the optional reflection questions.

Practice

Confession

We heal from sin by coming out of hiding. This is why this session, almost more than any other, must be put into practice. The practice of naming your sin to another person is what the writers of the Bible call "confession."

When we feel guilt and shame because of something we've done or not done, confession is likely the last thing we feel like doing.

But the path to being free from shame involves being open and transparent with someone we trust. In James 5v16 we read, "Confess your sins to each other and pray for each other so that you may be healed." When we name our sin or shame or secret with a trusted person, we can experience healing.

The practice is simple:

01 **Find someone you trust who will both love and accept you, *and* call you up to holiness. This could be a spiritual friend, community member, pastor, spiritual director, or therapist.**

02 **Find a place to meet that is private enough for you to feel safe and at peace.**

03 **Name your sin or shame or secret. Tell them the sin done by you, to you, or around you.**

04 **Let them love you, be faithful to you, and speak Jesus' forgiveness over you.**

For those of you *hearing* a confession, your role is very important. Don't shame or lecture or scold, just welcome in love.

Continue this practice on a regular basis, and keep the conversation going.

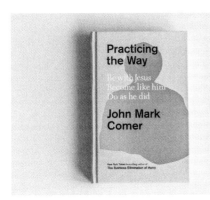

This session's reading

For this session, we're reading "Take up your cross," the final section of *Practicing the Way* by John Mark Comer, pp. 206-221.

Resources to go deeper

If you're interested in growing even more in your practice of confession, here are some more resources to consider.

Recommended reading

- *The Relational Soul* by Richard Plass and James Cofield
- *Not the Way It's Supposed to Be* by Cornelius Plantinga, Jr.

Recommended listening

- The Sin Series by Jon Tyson at Church of the City New York:
  link.practicingtheway.org/course-s6a
- The Bad Words video series by BibleProject: link.practicingtheway.org/course-s6b

Guest bio

Our guest this session was Jennie Allen. Jennie is an author, speaker, and the founder of IF:Gathering, an organization that exists to equip women with gospel-centered resources, events, and community as they disciple others. Learn more about Jennie and her work at ifgathering.com or check out her *New York Times* bestsellers, *Find Your People* and *Get Out of Your Head.*

Practice reflection

Reflection is a key component in our spiritual formation. Like practice, it allows what we learn to become a part of who we are.

Before your next time together, take five to ten minutes to journal out your answers to the following three questions.

01 **Where did you experience resistance in your practice of confession?**

02 **Where did you feel delight?**

03 **How does confession impact or change your view of God or yourself?**

Crafting a
Rule of Life

Overview

A Rule of Life is a schedule and a set of practices and relational rhythms that create space for us to be with Jesus, become like him, and do as he did. It's an intentional plan to slow down and simplify our life around being spiritually formed by Jesus. To turn the vision of spiritual formation into a reality.

It is an ancient idea, whose time has come again.

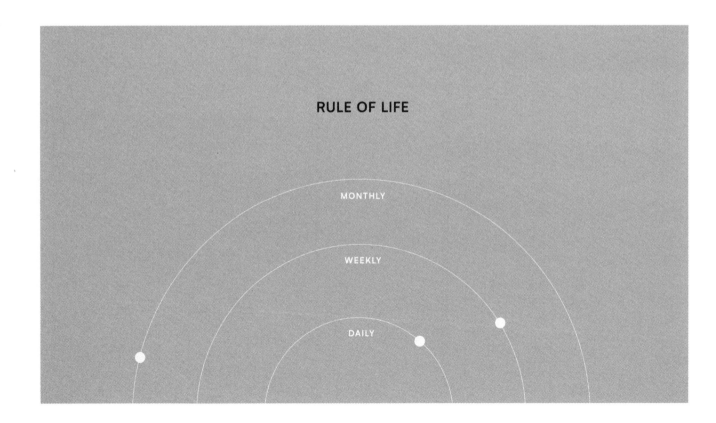

Practice reflection

Before we begin Session 07, break up into small groups and share your reflections on last session's exercise of confession.

01 **Where did you experience resistance in your practice of confession?**

02 **Where did you feel delight?**

03 **How does confession impact or change your view of God or yourself?**

Teaching

Scripture

I am the vine; you are the branches. If you remain in me and I in you, you will bear much fruit; apart from me you can do nothing. If you do not remain in me, you are like a branch that is thrown away and withers; such branches are picked up, thrown into the fire and burned. If you remain in me and my words remain in you, ask whatever you wish, and it will be done for you. This is to my Father's glory, that you bear much fruit, showing yourselves to be my disciples.

—John 15v5-8

Session summary

- Transformation is possible, but it's not inevitable.

- We need an intentional plan for our spiritual formation — what the early Christians called a "Rule of Life."

- A Rule of Life is a schedule and a set of practices and relational rhythms that create space for us to be with Jesus, become like him, and do as he did.

- When crafting a Rule for the first time, it's important to start small, and begin with subtraction, not addition.

- This coming week, our exercise is to design a Rule of Life.

Six tips

01   Start small

02   Think subtraction, not addition

03   Take a balanced approach

04   Take into account your personality and season of life

05   There is no formation without repetition

06   Do this in community

Teaching notes

As you watch Session 07 together, feel free to use this page to take notes.

Discussion questions

Pause the video and take some time to process together as a community.

Here are some questions for discussion:

01   What makes up your current Rule of Life?

02   As you think about designing a Rule of Life, how would you describe the spiritual needs of your personality and stage of life?

03   What practices do you want to include in your Rule of Life?

04   Who would be important to incorporate in the process of building your Rule of Life?

Practice notes

As you continue to watch Session 07 together, feel free to take notes here.

After the video

Closing prayer

End your time together by praying this liturgy:

Help us shape our lives, Father,
in the way of your Son —
the way of prayer and justice,
of generosity and purity,
of self-offering and compassion,
self-mastery and faith —
that the rhythms of our living
may be conduits of your grace,
welcoming your Kingdom in this world.
Amen.

OPTIONAL

If you'd like to continue your conversation, here are some additional questions
for reflection:

01 As you contemplate crafting a Rule of Life, what are some deep desires
that come up for you? What changes could bring more flourishing
to your life?

02 Imagine some practices you might tend to do individually. What would it
look like to experience these in community? What does it feel like in your
body to envision that?

Reflection notes

Feel free to use this page for notes on the optional reflection questions.

Practice

Crafting a Rule of Life

Now we're ready to take all the ideas we've been learning and "put it into practice" by writing our own Rule of Life.

There's no "right way" to craft a Rule of Life, and there's no one-size-fits-all approach to spiritual formation. The goal is to write a Rule that is customized for your unique personality, situation, and community.

To that end, we've created a digital tool called the Rule of Life Builder, which you can find on our website: www.practicingtheway.org/ruleoflifebuilder.

01 **Go to practicingtheway.org and log in.**

02 **Click on the Rule of Life Builder and follow its prompts. It will guide you through daily, weekly, monthly, and seasonal practices in a number of categories.**

03 **You can utilize the suggestions, write yours completely from scratch, or do a mix of both.**

- Remember: start small. Your Rule can begin with just a few small practices and rhythms.

- In this Course, we've covered three basic rhythms:

  ○ A daily **prayer** rhythm that includes the reading of **Scripture** in the quiet of **solitude**.

  ○ A weekly **Sabbath**.

  ○ And next session, we'll invite you to a weekly touchpoint in **community**.

- You can continue these practices and add, subtract, and edit as you sense the Spirit's direction.

- A Rule of Life isn't static, but dynamic. It changes with the seasons of our lives and stages of our discipleship. This digital template is easy to return to and modify. As time goes on, revisit your Rule and take the next step in your spiritual journey.

- You can do this exercise one time before the next session, or every day. It's also an exercise you can practice for the rest of your life, to open deeper and deeper parts of your inner world to God.

ACCESS THE RULE OF LIFE BUILDER
www.practicingtheway.org/ruleoflifebuilder

Resources to go deeper

If you're interested in growing even more in creating life-giving and communal rhythms in your life, here are some more resources to consider.

Recommended reading

- *God in My Everything* by Ken Shigematsu

- *At Home in the World* by Margaret Guenther

- *The Life We're Looking For* by our guest, Andy Crouch

Recommended listening

- Unhurrying with a Rule of Life series from Bridgetown Church:

  link.practicingtheway.org/course-s7a

- Unforced Rhythms of Grace teaching series from Bridgetown Church:

  bridgetown.church/series/unforced-rhythms

- John Mark's in-depth interview with Andy Crouch on a Rule of Life for the modern age:

  link.practicingtheway.org/course-s7b

- Episode 05 of the Practicing the Way podcast:

  link.practicingtheway.org/course-7c

Guest bio

Our guest this session was Andy Crouch, author, musician, journalist, and public speaker. Andy is a teacher and leader at Praxis, a venture-building organization advancing redemptive entrepreneurship in the for-profit and nonprofit sectors. To learn more about Andy and his work, visit andy-crouch.com.

Practice reflection

Reflection is a key component in our spiritual formation. Like practice, it allows what we learn to become a part of who we are.

Before your next time together, take five to ten minutes to journal out your answers to the following three questions.

01   Share about your process of creating a Rule of Life. What worked for you?

02   What feelings came up for you as you worked through this exercise?

03   What do you anticipate will be the most life-giving and transformative practice you came up with?

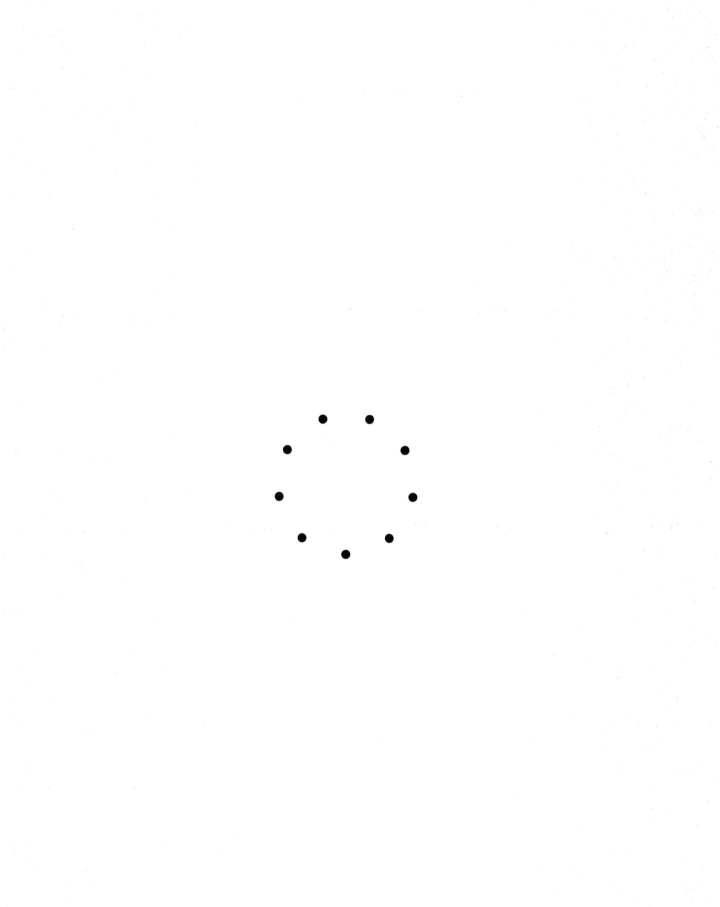

Rule of Life resources

A Rule of Life from Practicing the Way

01   A community of rest in a culture of hurry and exhaustion, through the practice of **Sabbath.**

02   A community of peace and quiet in a culture of anxiety and noise, through the practice of **solitude.**

03   A community of communion with God in a culture of distraction and escapism, through the practice of **prayer.**

04   A community of love and depth in a culture of individualism and superficiality, through the practice of **community.**

05   A community of courageous fidelity to orthodoxy in a culture of ideological compromise, through the practice of **Scripture.**

06   A community of holiness in a culture of indulgence and immorality, through the practice of **fasting.**

07   A community of contentment in a culture of consumerism, through the practice of **generosity.**

08   A community of justice, mercy, and reconciliation in a culture of injustice and division, through the practice of **service.**

09   A community of hospitality in a culture of hostility, through the practice of **witness.**

Sample Rule of Life 01

FROM PRACTICING THE WAY

	SABBATH	PRAYER	FASTING	SOLITUDE	GENEROSITY	SCRIPTURE	COMMUNITY	SERVICE	WITNESS
DAILY		Prayer rhythm		A time in silence to begin and end the day		Reading Scripture			
WEEKLY	Sabbath day to stop, rest, delight, and worship		Fast until sundown				A meal together and worship on Sunday		
MONTHLY/SEASONALLY					Giving 10 percent of your income, with special attention to the church and the poor			An act of service to the poor with the aim of kinship	An act of hospitality and regularly praying for one person in your life who does not know Jesus

Sample Rule of Life 02[*]

BRITTANY'S RULE — GRADUATE STUDENT IN HER TWENTIES

———————————

* Adapted from *God in My Everything* by Ken Shigematsu

	SABBATH	PRAYER	FASTING	SOLITUDE	GENEROSITY	SCRIPTURE	COMMUNITY	SERVICE	WITNESS
DAILY		Spend time with God in prayer				Spend time with God through Bible study			
WEEKLY	Take a Sabbath each Sunday						Participate in church at the Sunday evening service and at young adults group on Monday night		
MONTHLY/SEASONALLY				Reflect on how I am meeting my goals / living my rule and where I need to grow	Tithe		Connect with my peer-mentor / spiritual friend		

Sample Rule of Life 03*

JUNE'S RULE — MARRIED WITH A YOUNG SON, WORKS AS A TEACHER

* Adapted from *God in My Everything* by Ken Shigematsu

	SABBATH	PRAYER	FASTING	SOLITUDE	GENEROSITY	SCRIPTURE	COMMUNITY	SERVICE	WITNESS
DAILY		As I can, pray throughout the day — in the car, on a walk, before mealtimes				Read Scripture at night before I go to bed; as I can, pray through these Scriptures the following day			
WEEKLY	Rest and Sunday worship, typically on a Saturday or Sunday (depending on what is going on)						Small group with families with young children (currently working through a Bible study book on parenting)		
MONTHLY/SEASONALLY	Travel once a year in the summertime				Tithe every month Support missionaries and other charitable organizations every month				Through friendship and invite people to church and through our Easter and Christmas outreaches

Life Together

Overview

"If you want to go fast, go alone, but if you want to go far, go together." We are not designed to travel the spiritual journey by ourselves. We need community to practice the Way.

And Jesus' call to community goes far beyond church attendance to relationships of depth, vulnerability, and a commitment to transformation.

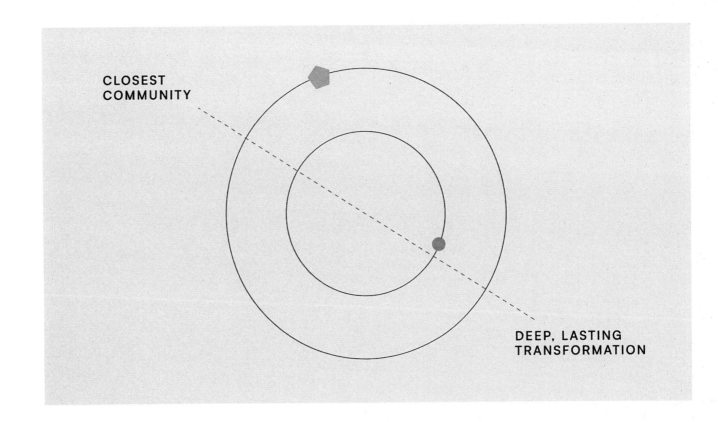

CLOSEST
COMMUNITY

DEEP, LASTING
TRANSFORMATION

Practice reflection

Before we begin Session 08, break up into small groups and share your reflections on last session's exercise of creating a Rule of Life.

01 Share about your process of creating a Rule of Life. What worked for you?

02 What feelings came up for you as you worked through this exercise?

03 What do you anticipate will be the most life-giving and transformative practice you came up with?

Teaching

Scripture

A crowd was sitting around him, and they told him, "Your mother and brothers are outside looking for you." "Who are my mother and my brothers?" he asked. Then he looked at those seated in a circle around him and said, "Here are my mother and my brothers! Whoever does God's will is my brother and sister and mother."

—Mark 3v32-35

Session summary

- Jesus' invitation was to come and do life together.

- Through Jesus, we have been adopted into the family of God.

- Jesus' desire is not just to form you into a person of love, but to form a community of love.

- You can't follow Jesus alone; spiritual formation is a relational process.

- Four layers of community:*

  - Intimates: 1-5 people who deeply know and love us

  - Friends: 15 people with whom we do life

  - Village: 150 people, the maximum we can be in relationship with

  - Tribe: The larger group we identify with and belong to

- Spiritual friendships are marked by three core characteristics:

  - Depth

  - Vulnerability

  - Commitment to transformation

- Our final practice is to cultivate a community of spiritual friendship and begin meeting regularly.

---

* Robin Dunbar, "Coevolution of Neocortical Size, Group Size and Language in Humans," *Behavioral and Brain Sciences* 16, no. 4 (1993).

Teaching notes

As you watch Session 08 together, feel free to use this page to take notes.

Discussion questions

Pause the video and take some time to process together as a community.

Here are some questions for discussion:

01 Of the three relational characteristics named (depth, vulnerability, and a commitment to transformation), which is the hardest for you?

02 As you reflect on your life and relationships, who has been or could be a "soul friend" to you on this spiritual formation journey?

03 What has Jesus done in your life over the last eight sessions, during our time together?

04 What's your next step in your spiritual journey, your "next right thing"?

Practice notes

After the video

Closing prayer

End your time together by praying this liturgy:

Lord Jesus,
There is no greater prayer than yours —
make us one as you are one,
in devotion, in living, in love.
Amen.

OPTIONAL

If you'd like to continue your conversation, here are some additional questions
for reflection:

01 What comes up when you consider meeting in an intentional community?

02 What natural pathways exist in your life for this, whether within your
church or other spaces?

03 As you examine your own desires, what do you envision for your time?
Engaging in a Practice? Reading a book? Taking a BibleProject class?
Meeting for a meal or prayer? Or something else?

Reflection notes

Feel free to use this page for notes on the optional reflection questions.

Practice

Do life in community

Jesus' call to community isn't a theory or an idea, it's a practice — a relational way of doing life together.

Jesus would preach to crowds of thousands, but he spent most of his time with a small circle of disciples, in homes and around tables.

It's important to worship in church on Sunday and be part of a larger community, but it's just as important to know and name your "twelve" and your "three." To cultivate spiritual friendships that last for years.

So our final practice is to identify our intentional community and begin to meet with them regularly.

01   **Identify a community to meet with regularly.**

02   **This community could be with just one or two others, or a dozen or even more.**

03   **We recommend you meet weekly, but it could be biweekly or monthly.**

04   **We also recommend you share a meal when you meet. The act of "breaking bread" is central to the Christian way. Something powerful happens when we eat together.**

- But remember, there's no one "right" model for you to follow. You may choose a house church with 20 kids running around a backyard on a Sunday afternoon or a small triad for group spiritual direction early in the morning.

- We encourage you to follow the pathway of your church — whether in a small group, table community, or house church, or a women's or men's Bible study.

- You could follow this Course with any of the nine Practices available from Practicing the Way, share a weekly meal and pray for one another, or work through more free resources from BibleProject, like the following:

  - Reflections mini-cast with discussion questions: bibleproject.com/podcasts/reflections

  - Reading plans: bibleproject.com/reading-plans

  - Heavier classes: bibleproject.com/classroom

Resources to go deeper

If you're interested in learning more about doing life in community, here are some more resources to consider.

Recommended reading

- *When the Church Was a Family* by Joseph Hellerman
- *The Connected Life* by Todd Hall
- *Made to Belong* by David Kim

Recommended listening

- The Community Practice teaching series from Bridgetown Church: link.practicingtheway.org/course-s8

Additional resources

- The Community Practice from Practicing the Way: practicingtheway.org/community (coming soon). If you'd like to learn more about the practice of community, you can run the Community Practice, a four-session experience designed to integrate the practice of community into your regular life.

Guest bio

Our guest this session was Reverend Dr. Charlie Dates, pastor of Salem Baptist Church of Chicago. He is a speaker, professor, and author. Check out his contribution in the book *Say It!: Celebrating Expository Preaching in the African American Tradition*, or listen to him preach at salemchicago.org.

Practice reflection

Reflection is a key component in our spiritual formation. Like practice, it allows what we learn to become a part of who we are.

For your final reflection in this course, take five to ten minutes to journal out your answers to the following two questions.

01 As you think back over this Course, what is sticking with you most?

02 Take a moment to remember how you felt when you first started this Course. What has changed in how you feel or think? How do you see yourself or God differently? Do you notice any change or growth?

PART 03

Continue the Journey

The Practices

Information alone isn't enough to produce transformation.

By adopting not just the teaching but the practices from Jesus' own life, we open up our entire being to God and allow him to transform us into people of love.

Our nine core Practices work together to form a Rule of Life for the modern era.

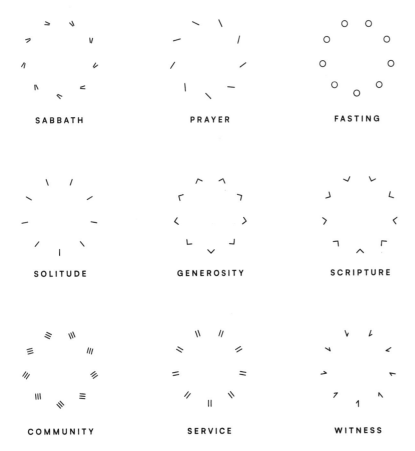

SABBATH

PRAYER

FASTING

SOLITUDE

GENEROSITY

SCRIPTURE

COMMUNITY

SERVICE

WITNESS

Each Practice includes:

Four Sessions

Each session includes teaching, guided discussion, and weekly exercises to integrate the Practices into daily life.

Companion Guide

A detailed guide with question prompts, session-by-session exercises, and space to write and reflect.

Recommended Resources

Additional recommended readings and podcasts to get the most out of the Practices.

Recommended Reading

Books on spiritual formation

- *The Ruthless Elimination of Hurry* by John Mark Comer
- *The Renovation of the Heart* by Dallas Willard
- *The Great Omission* by Dallas Willard
- *Invitation to a Journey* by M. Robert Mulholland
- *The Deeply Formed Life* by Rich Villodas
- *Emotionally Healthy Spirituality* by Pete Scazzero
- *The Relational Soul* by Richard Plass and James Cofield
- *Sacred Fire* by Ronald Rolheiser

Books on solitude and silence

- *Invitation to Solitude and Silence* by Ruth Haley Barton
- *The Way of the Heart* by Henri Nouwen
- *The Power of Silence* by Robert Cardinal Sarah

Books on prayer

- *Praying Like Monks, Living Like Fools* by Tyler Staton
- *Armchair Mystic* by Mark Thibodeaux
- *Prayer* by Richard Foster
- *The Spiritual Life* by Evelyn Underhill
- *The Shattered Lantern* by Ronald Rolheiser
- *Time for God* by Jacques Philippe

Books on Scripture

- *Shaped by the Word* by M. Robert Mulholland
- *Eat This Book* by Eugene Peterson

Books on Sabbath

- *Sabbath* by Dan Allender
- *Keeping the Sabbath Wholly* by Marva J. Dawn
- *The Sabbath* by Abraham Joshua Heschel
- *Subversive Sabbath* by A.J. Swoboda

Books on community

- *When the Church Was a Family* by Joseph Hellerman
- *The Connected Life* by Todd Hall
- *Made to Belong* by David Kim
- *Life Together* by Dietrich Bonhoeffer

Books on a Rule of Life

- *God in My Everything* by Ken Shigematsu
- *At Home in the World* by Margaret Guenther

Devotional reading

- *A Testament of Devotion* by Thomas Kelly
- *With* by Skye Jethani
- *Interior Freedom*, *Time for God*, and *Searching for and Maintaining Peace* by Jacques Philippe
- *The Pursuit of God* by A.W. Tozer
- *Experiencing the Trinity* by Darrell Johnson
- *Christian Perfection* by François Fénelon

The Circle

Practicing the Way is a nonprofit that develops spiritual formation resources for churches and small groups learning how to become apprentices in the Way of Jesus.

We believe one of the greatest needs of our time is for people to discover how to become lifelong disciples of Jesus. To that end, we help people learn how to be with Jesus, become like him, and do as he did, through the practices and rhythms he and his earliest followers lived by.

All of our downloadable ministry resources are available at no cost, thanks to the generosity of The Circle and other givers from around the world who partner with us to see formation integrated into the Church at large.

To learn more or join us, visit practicingtheway.org/give.

To inquire about ordering this Companion Guide
in bulk quantities for your church,
small group, or staff, contact
churches@penguinrandomhouse.com.